Contents

Some words are printed in bold, **like this.** You can find out what they mean by looking in the glossary, on page 46.

Dance of the people

Have you ever watched Appalachian clog dancers tap-dancing to an old time American tune? Perhaps you have seen Morris dancers jumping and bashing sticks together on a village green, or Scottish dancers in kilts springing over a pair of crossed swords? These are the sorts of things that people usually think of as folk dancing. In fact, folk dance is far more varied than this. There are simple dances with easy steps that everyone can learn, and fiendishly difficult dances that take years to perfect. There are slow, stately dances and fierce, spinning and leaping dances. There are hat dances from Mexico and frog dances from the Baltic countries. There are dances where people imitate animals, and story dances with strange characters such as **hobby horses**, clowns and doctors.

▼ Morris dancers in Tideswell, Derbyshire. Tideswell is a processional Morris dance. This means that the dancers move from place to place. There are records of Morris dancing in Tideswell from as early as 1797.

C...   nd
F...   e

Andrew Solway

www.heinemannlibrary.co.uk
Visit our website to find out more information about **Heinemann Library** books.

To order:
 Phone 44 (0) 1865 888066
 Send a fax to 44 (0) 1865 314091
 Visit the Heinemann Bookshop at www.heinemannlibrary.co.uk to browse our catalogue and order online.

Heinemann Library is an imprint of Capstone Global Library Limited, a company incorporated in England and Wales having its registered office at 7 Pilgrim Street, London, EC4V 6LB – Registered company number: 6695582

Heinemann is a registered trademark of Pearson Education Limited, under licence to Capstone Global Library Limited

Editorial: Sarah Shannon and Robyn Hardyman
Design: Steve Mead and Geoff Ward
Picture Research: Maria Joannou
Illustration: Sarah Kelley
Production: Duncan Gilbert

Originated by Modern Age Repro House Ltd
Printed and bound by Leo Paper Products

ISBN 978 0431 933 146 (Hardback)
12 11 10 09 08
10 9 8 7 6 5 4 3 2 1

ISBN 978 0431 933 221 (Paperback)
14 13 12 11 10
10 9 8 7 6 5 4 3 2 1

British Library Cataloguing in Publication Data
Solway, Andrew
    Country and folk. - (Dance)
    793.3'1

A full catalogue record for this book is available from the British Library.

Acknowledgements
The publishers would like to thank the following for permission to reproduce photographs: © Alamy Images pp. **5** (Richard Levine), **7** (AGRfoto/Alex Rowbotham), **14** (Pictures Colour Library), **15** (Simon Hathaway), **16-17** (Jupiterimages/Agence Images), **21** (Peter Titmuss), **26** (Julie Marland), **31** (ilian travel), **32** (imagebroker), **39** (Jon Arnold Images Ltd), **42** (Chuck Place); © Corbis pp. **4** (Adam Woolfitt), **12** (Jason Lee/ Reuters), **27** (Floris Leeuwenberg/The Cover Story), **34** (Jon Sparks), **37** (Anton Meres/ Reuters), **40** (Baldev); © Digital Light Source p. **30** (Jacob Hutchings Photography); © Getty Images pp. **10** (Reportage/ Homer Sykes), **24** (Christopher Furlong), **28** (Fritz Goro/Time Life Pictures), **35** (China Photos), **36** (Tim Boyle); © Lonely Planet Images p. **11** (Shannon Nace); © Photographers Direct pp. **20** (Frank Lavelle Photography), **43** (Gail Ward Photography); © Photolibrary p. **22** (Nordic Photos); © Rex Features pp. **9** (Sipa Press), **19** (Nick Cunard); © Topham Picturepoint p. **18** (Josef Polleross /The Image Works).

Cover photograph of line dancing reproduced with permission of © Photoshot/PYMCA.

Every effort has been made to contact copyright holders of any material reproduced in this book. Any omissions will be rectified in subsequent printings if notice is given to the publishers.

Dance Facts

What *is* a folk dance?

There are so many kinds of folk dance that it is hard to say exactly what a folk dance is.

Folk dancing is *not*…

- classical dance. Classical dance uses techniques such as ballet from Europe, or Kathakali dance from India. They are dances that were made originally for performing at court, or religious dances performed in temples.
- modern dance, or other kinds of 'art' dance. These are dances made by choreographers for performing in theatres or other performance venues.

Folk dancing *is*…

- usually social. Dances are nearly always for groups of people to do together.
- made for a particular occasion, often something that happens each year. However, today people often mix together dances that were made for different occasions and that come from different places.

▼ Today, folk dances from many countries are often performed at festivals and celebrations. This woman is performing a Korean folk dance at a festival in New York.

What are folk dances about?

Today, people do folk dance classes for fun, or dance at celebrations or special ceremonies. Some people are **professional** folk dancers, who perform in theatres and at festivals. However, most folk dances were not originally made to be performed in front of an audience. In the past, they had a serious purpose. People danced to ensure the success of next year's crops, or to help them work together on an important job. Some dances were made to defend a community from storms, disease or evil spirits.

Dances from the past

Sometimes modern folk dances seem meaningless. But if we look into their history, it helps us understand why people started doing them. We can find out about ancient dances from old pictures and sculptures, and from descriptions written hundreds of years ago.

The earliest dances?

The earliest people got food by hunting animals and gathering fruits and other kinds of plants. The oldest paintings we know of, found in caves, mostly show the animals that people hunted at the time. Dances that represented hunting or animals were probably the first kinds of dance that people did. Many folk dances today imitate animals or hunting. However, these are not the direct **descendants** of the earliest animal and hunting dances.

The cycle of seasons

For hundreds of years, most people were farmers or worked on the land, growing food and raising animals. The cycle of seasons was very important to them. A long winter, an early frost or a severe dry season could ruin crops, kill animals and leave people starving. Dancing was part of a cycle of celebrations and **rituals** to ensure good **harvests**.

The most important dances in the cycle were at the start and end of winter. Many of these dances were about death and rebirth. The old year died, marking the start of winter, and the new year was reborn. At one time, it is thought that these rituals involved human **sacrifice**, in which a 'king' was killed each year, and his blood was scattered on the fields to ensure that the next year's crops were good. Later the human sacrifice became an animal sacrifice, and eventually this became a dance about death and rebirth.

Towards the end of winter, dances were part of rituals to banish winter and hasten the arrival of spring. These dances often involved jumping as high as possible, to encourage the crops to grow high. Many of the folk dances that still happen around Easter time, or early in the year, have echoes of these early rituals.

▲ These maypole dancers are in South Tyrol, in the Italian Alps. As in most European countries, they are dancing round the maypole on May Day (1 May). In Sweden, however, maypole dancing is a midsummer ceremony.

Gods and spirits

When people are about to do something challenging, such as take an exam, go on a long trip or take part in a sports competition, they often ask people to wish them luck. In the past, people asked gods and spirits to bring them luck, and they often did this by dancing. They also made dances of another kind to keep away bad luck, by scaring off evil spirits.

Few modern folk dances are directly connected with religious ceremonies. However, many are descendants of earlier dances that either asked for blessings from the gods or tried to frighten away evil spirits. In maypole dances, for instance, coloured ribbons are tied to a tall pole, and people weave in and out as they dance around the pole (see page 23). In Austria, the maypole is often a tree with the lower branches chopped off. Experts think that originally maypole dances were dances to the gods of the forest, to ask for their blessing. The Chinese lion dance, which is performed at Chinese New Year, involves wearing red clothes and setting off loud firecrackers. The colour and loud noises are meant to keep away evil spirits and give the New Year a good start.

The English Dancing Master

John Playford was a bookseller and publisher in London in the 17th century. In 1651, he published a book called *The English Dancing Master*. It included music for 105 folk tunes, and instructions for a dance to go with each of the tunes. Playford produced seven editions (versions) of *The English Dancing Master* before he died in 1686.

Each new edition had extra dances and tunes. New editions of the book continued to come out until 1728. Most of the dances in the first edition were folk dances that had existed for many years before Playford published his book. However, many of the dances and tunes added in later editions were made up for the book.

Reviving dances

Although many folk dances go back hundreds of years, not all of them have been danced continuously over this period. Some dances were banned by religious leaders because they involved worshipping gods and spirits rather than following the common religion. Many Muslims, and some Puritan Christians, thought that all kinds of dancing were bad.

Other dances were stopped because they were part of a custom that became too wild and rowdy. These were often customs that involved dancers going from house to house, asking for food or presents. In some places the dancers started getting drunk, and demanding drink or money at the houses they visited.

Amazing Fact

Abbots Bromley Horn Dance

It is difficult to date many folk dances accurately. However, there is scientific evidence to show that the Abbots Bromley Horn Dance is very old. It is performed in the village of Abbots Bromley, in Staffordshire, England, early in September. There are 12 dancers, and 6 of them carry large reindeer antlers on their shoulders. Carbon dating has shown that the antlers are almost 1000 years old.

Technique

Spinning dances

Generally dance is not an important part of Muslim religion. However, for one group of Muslims, known as Sufis, music and dance are part of the worship of Allah (God). The whirling dervish dance of Turkey is the best-known kind of Sufi dancing. However, there are other kinds, such as Gnawa dance and music from Morocco. In Sufi dancing, the dancers spin for long periods of time, often going into a trance-like state.

▲ The Mevlevi Muslims of Turkey are better known as whirling dervishes. Their dance is a religious ceremony to remember Allah (God).

Traditionally, Morris dances were danced only by men. However, when Cecil Sharp revived folk dance in the early 20th century, ladies formed Morris groups as well as men.

In the late 19th century, people in many countries became interested in reviving old customs and traditions. The English musician Cecil Sharp began to collect folk dances in 1899, after he saw a Morris dance performance near Oxford in England. At the time, folk dances had almost died out in England. Sharp published a book of Morris dances and another of sword dances from northern England. The interest he created led to a revival of folk dances and customs in Britain.

Biography

Lloyd 'Pappy' Shaw

The 'Cecil Sharp' of American square dancing (see page 18) was a high school superintendent called Lloyd 'Pappy' Shaw. In the 1920s he realized that square dancing was in decline. The 'callers', who tell the dancers what steps to do, were all elderly, and they were not passing on the dances they knew to the next generation. Shaw therefore travelled the country speaking to all the elderly callers, writing down their dances. He published the dances in a book called *Cowboy Dances*. Shaw also trained young square dance teams in his school.

Sharp was not the only person to revive old folk traditions. When he visited America, he met a woman called Olive Dame Campbell, and helped her to collect dances and music in the Appalachian Mountain region. In Hungary at about the same time, the composers Béla Bartók and Zoltán Kodály toured the rural areas of Eastern Europe collecting folk music. In South America during the 1950s, the government of Bolivia encouraged people to rescue the folk music and dance of the original people of the Andes, before the Spanish invaded South America in the 1500s. Andean folk musicians play drums, panpipes, flutes and a small kind of mandolin called a charango. Andean dances range from Mexican-style hat dances (see page 35) to rhythmic dances with hip movements and fast footwork that are similar to some kinds of African dance.

▼ Dancers in traditional Andean costume at the Virgen de la Candelaria Festival in Puno, Peru. The festival lasts for 18 days in February. During that time, Puno is the folk dance capital of South America.

Celebrations and weddings

Today, folk dancing is not always linked to traditional customs and **rituals.** Some people go to folk dance societies and clubs to learn folk dances, and others perform folk dances professionally. However, there are still many folk dances that are particular to a place or to a group of people. Some happen at certain times of the year, to fit in with the cycle of the seasons. Others are part of celebrations and special occasions that happen year-round, such as weddings and births.

New Year dances

New Year dances are usually concerned with keeping away evil and bringing good luck for the coming year. The Chinese lion dance (see page 35) is one New Year's dance. Another is the *capra*, a dance from Romania. The dancers are dressed as different animals,

▶ The lion dance is a traditional part of New Year celebrations in China. The tradition is over a thousand years old. The photo shows lion dancers in Beijing.

and one of them is the *capra* (goat). When the dancers meet people in the street, they make a circle around them and dance. They then collect money as a reward. This dance clearly reflects old beliefs in magic circles, which bring luck or protection to the people within them. (For more on circle dances, see page 16.)

Eggs and more maypoles

Spring festivals can take place as early as March or as late as May. At Easter there are often dances with eggs. In Austria, egg dancing involves manoeuvring eggs into a basket using only the feet. There is also an English egg dance which involves dancing blindfold on a floor dotted with eggs.

Maypole dances are part of many spring festivals. However, they also happen at other times of year. In the Czech Republic, for example, there are maypole dances at midsummer, and afterwards the maypole is burned on a bonfire.

Amazing Fact

Fire dances

In Celtic countries there were eight fire festivals each year – four sun festivals and four moon festivals. At the original festivals, humans were sacrificed in the fires. At the Beltane fire festival, in early May, dancers jump high over the fire to ensure good crops.

There are also fire dances in many other countries. In Bulgaria, the fire dance involves walking on hot coals. In Papua New Guinea, fire dancers walk through fires wearing huge masks made from bamboo and bark cloth. There is also a fire dance from Rajasthan, India, in which women dance with a pot of flaming coals on their head. In the dance they spin, sit and stand up again, all without tipping up the fire pot.

Autumn

Late summer and autumn is the time for **harvest** festivals and dances. The Puck fair, which happens in some parts of Ireland in August, is an early harvest celebration. During the fair, a decorated goat is tethered on a platform, and for three days people dance around it. In the past, the goat was probably **sacrificed** as part of the celebration. Another scary harvest dance from Lithuania involves a circle of men, with a girl in the centre of the circle holding an axe. The girl throws the axe into the air, and whoever catches it is entitled to a kiss.

▲ These people are circle dancing at a wedding in Scorieu, Romania.

Winter

Midwinter celebrations include fire festivals (see page 13) and dances about death and **resurrection**. In the Polish dance 'Matthew is dead', for instance, a man dies and is put into a coffin for his funeral. However, he loves dancing so much that when the funeral dances begin, he jumps out of his coffin and joins in.

Weddings and other celebrations

People dance at weddings in every part of the world. Often the dances are about bringing the married couple good luck and a large family. In northern Italy, sword dances were part of wedding ceremonies, to clear away evil spirits before the wedding. In Slovakia the wedding celebration involves several circle dances. In one, the chief bridesmaid stands in the middle of the circle cradling a plate as if it was a baby. She then collects money from the wedding guests for any children that the married couple may have.

Some dances are used on many different occasions. The *hora*, a Romanian circle dance, is danced at just about every possible celebration or social event. At weddings, the guests dance around the bride in a large circle at her house, before the ceremony. During the ceremony itself, the bride and groom are crowned with marriage **wreaths**, then they dance a *hora* around the church altar with the priest and their parents.

Dance Facts

Carnival

Carnival is a big celebration that happens in countries around the world during February or March. The Mardi Gras celebrations in New Orleans and the carnivals in Rio de Janeiro and Trinidad are the best-known carnivals, but there are hundreds of others.

The highlight of most carnivals is a huge procession. People dance through the streets in costumes and masks, or ride on large decorated floats. Some carnival celebrations also involve battle dances in which spring overcomes winter.

◀ The most colourful and vibrant carnival celebrations happen in Latin America. This carnival is in Asunción, Paraguay.

Circles, lines and couples

Folk dances are usually group dances, and they are organized into patterns. The first folk dances were probably danced in a circle. Circle dances are found in most cultures around the world. Another early kind of folk dance was the chain dance, which is a circle broken in one place. Later came dances in lines and other patterns. As folk dancing developed, the patterns became more complicated. In these early dances, men and women usually danced separately. Dances in which men and women danced together in couples came later.

Circle and chain dances

The circle has always been associated with magic. Circle dances were often part of religious ceremonies or **rituals**, where centre of the circle was a 'magic space' protected from evil. The centre could contain a maypole or a bonfire, or be a space for **solo** dancers to show their skill.

In Europe there are many circle dances, from the Spanish *sardana* in the west to the *kolo* in Eastern Europe. An ancient American circle dance is the sun dance. This was held once a year by Native Americans from the North American Plains until the 19th century. The dance was a religious ritual that went on for several days.

Chain dances are closely related to circle dances. The dancers in the chain may link hands, or they may hold either end of a stick or handkerchief.

Couple dances

Couple dances are ones in which a man and a woman, or a girl and a boy, dance together. Many ballroom dances, such as the polka and the waltz, are **descendants** of folk dances for couples. The polka is a Czech dance step that is part of many folk dances (see page 20). The waltz is a more refined version of a German or Austrian turning dance called a *ländler*.

Most couple dances began as **courtship** dances. These kinds of dances are often a sort of story: the boy or man comes boldly up to the girl or woman, who rejects him or acts shy. Eventually the female is won over, and the two dance together.

▼ The sardana is a circle dance from the Pyrenees mountains, on the border between France and Spain. Dancers link hands and dance with their arms raised. The circle grows bigger as more people join in.

Sets and squares

As couple dances became more popular, the couples began to be organized into circles, lines and other groupings. Most of the country dances that people do today are dances of this kind. The dancers are often organised into 'sets' of a fixed number of couples.

In American square dancing, there are four couples, one on each side of a square. In traditional square dances, the first couple does a 'figure' (a set of steps). The second couple then moves on round the square and does the figure with the third and then the fourth couple. Next comes a chorus in which all the couples dance together. Then the second couple become the leading couple and the dance begins again. A caller controls the overall dance by calling out the names of the steps the dancers should do.

▲ Line dancing is another kind of American dance that has become even more popular than square dancing. Modern line dancing is a kind of social dance rather than folk dancing.

Technique

Square dance moves

Circle family. All the dancers in the square join hands to form a circle, and move forward around the circle. The caller will say how far round the circle should go (full circle, half circle etc.).

Dosado. Two couples are facing each other. They step towards each other and pass right shoulders with their opposite number. Without turning, each dancer goes round their opposite number and back to their place.

Allemande. Each dancer in a couple faces towards the nearest dancer in the couple next to them (their 'corner'). Dancers turn their corners by the left forearm. Each dancer ends facing his or her own partner again.

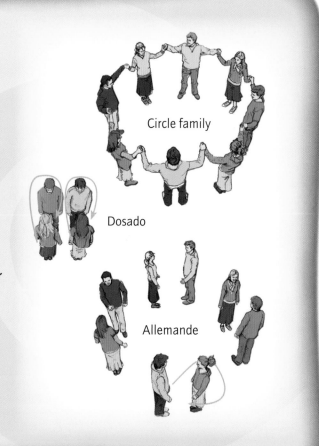

Circle family

Dosado

Allemande

Today, modern Western square dancing is more popular than traditional square dance. It is more complex, because all four couples dance at once, and there are many more steps to learn. Dancers who do Western square dancing must learn the steps carefully so that they can follow the caller's instructions immediately.

Longways sets

Another common grouping is the longways set. The set is made up of two lines of people, with men on one side and women on the other. The couple at the head of the set normally lead the dancing, or dance while the others watch. There is then usually a section where everyone moves around, and a new couple becomes the lead. Longways sets are found in the dances of many countries. They were especially popular in England during the 16th and 17th centuries. American contra dances are similar to English longways dances. As in square dancing there is a dance caller, who tells the dancers which move to do next.

▼ Scottish country dancing is similar to English country dancing. The couple in the centre are the lead couple in this longways set.

Stepping out

Many folk dances are designed for anyone to join in, so the steps are fairly simple. But this isn't always the case. Some kinds of folk dance have tricky steps and complicated rhythms. They give talented dancers the chance to show off their skills.

International steps

Some steps are common to folk dances from many different parts of the world. Often the steps are quite simple ones, such as skips, gallops, and the side step (side-together-side). Two other step patterns that have become popular are the waltz and the polka. The waltz step is a down-up-up turning step. It comes originally from the Austrian/German *ländler* folk dance, but it is also found in other dances. Polka steps have found their way into even more dances than the waltz. The dancer does a step-together-step, with sometimes a turn or a hop at the end. Today there are polka steps in folk dances from Finland to South America.

▶ Today the waltz is a ballroom dance, but its roots are in a folk dance, the Austrian *ländler*.

▲ In Russian *plyaska* dancing the men improvise acrobatic solos.

Strutting their stuff

Not all folk dance steps are easy. Some, such as Irish step dances and Appalachian clogging, are like tap dancing (see pages 36–7). Scottish sword dancing (see page 25) and the Spanish fandango both involve very fast, complex footwork that takes years to learn well. Many Balkan folk dances, and some Spanish dances, are difficult because they combine complex footwork with unusual rhythms.

Some dances are difficult because they have lots of high leaps and turns. English Morris dancing includes high leaps, and many Russian folk dances involve turns and impressive jumping. Sometimes the basic dance has fairly simple steps, but there are opportunities in the dance for people to really show off. Basque dances, from the Pyrenees Mountains between France and Spain, often have sections where dancers really go to town with high kicks and leaps.

Most folk dances have set steps, but sometimes a soloist can **improvise**. Russian *plyaska* dances include many different steps, but the dancers improvise the way they put them together. Often these dances are competitions between two dancers (traditionally men).

Stepping styles

Dance steps can be done in many different ways. In some dances they are smooth and gliding, in others the dancers move fast and energetically. There is some evidence that the style of a folk dance is related to the geography of the area where the dance is made. In a warm place with gentle, rolling countryside, the dances are often smooth and gentle, with no fast or strong movements. In harsher landscapes, such as mountain areas or dry regions, the dancing is often faster and involves leaps and turns.

These differences can be seen in the folk-dance styles of Denmark, Sweden and Norway. Although the dances of the three countries have similar steps and patterns, the landscapes are very different, and so are the dance styles.

▲ The hambo is a traditional Swedish dance. It is in a three-beat rhythm, like the waltz.

Denmark is a gentle, open landscape with rich farmland, low hills and few trees. Danish folk dance is also gentle and easy-going. The dances are mainly for groups and couples and are simple enough for everyone to join in.

Sweden has many forests and lakes, and northern Sweden has cold, bleak winters. Many Swedish dances are designed for large gatherings, as with Danish dances, but there is more energy and liveliness in them. Swedish dance music is often played by groups of violins rather than single instruments, which gives energy to the dancing.

Maypole weaving

In the oldest kind of maypole dance, which is still performed in parts of Sweden and Germany, there are no ribbons on the maypole. Ribbon dances were introduced in England in the 18th century. The dancers work together to weave a pattern in the ribbons, then usually reverse the dance to unweave the ribbons.

There are many different kinds of maypole weaving. In the grand chain dance, alternate dancers go in opposite directions and weave in and out of each other. The result is a sort of plait or braid on the pole. In the barbers' pole dance, the girls dance once round the pole, and then the boys, and so on. The result is a spiral pattern of ribbons. In the gypsy's tent dance, partners dance around each other to plait together a sort of tent of ribbons that is not wrapped around the pole. In the spider's web dance, dancers form a web around the pole.

The landscape of Norway is harsher than that of either Sweden or Denmark. There are steep mountains, deep fjords and dense forests. Norwegian dances are mainly couple dances in which the man and the woman have very different steps. The woman moves gently, always turning, while the man improvises a strong, acrobatic **solo** around her. In one dance, called the *halling*, the woman carries the man's hat on a pole. Near the end of the dance the man leaps up and kicks his hat off the pole.

Technique

Some country dance steps

The following steps are found in English country dances and American contra dances.

- *Single*. Two steps in any direction, ending with the feet closed.
- *Double*. Four steps forward or back, ending with the feet closed.
- *Swing*. Two people turning together quickly, holding both hands.
- *Sides*. Two dancers (usually partners) go forward in four counts to meet side by side, then back in four counts to where they started.
- *Three hands star*. Two dancers join hands, and a third dancer puts their hand on top. Dancers move in the direction they face.
- *Hey*. Two groups of dancers, moving in single file and in opposite directions, weave in and out of each other.

Sword dances

Lots of folk dances seem to be about fighting. There are dances where partners seem to slap and hit each other, and where they carry sticks, swords, axes, and even guns. Many of these weapons dances were not originally about fighting, but were ancient religious **rituals**.

▲ The Britannia Coconut Dancers perform every April in Bacup, Lancashire, UK. Their dances include a 'sword dance' using half-hoops of flowers rather than swords. Their faces are painted to ward off evil spirits and may also reflect a link to coal mining.

Swords and sticks

Sword dances are found all over the world. There are many different versions. In some places, the swords have been banned because of the danger, and the dancers use sticks.

There are several different types of sword dance. Perhaps the most common are 'point and hilt' dances, where the dancers hold the hilt of their own sword and the point of their neighbour's to make a chain or a circle. These dances also usually involve sections where the dancers clash together their swords or sticks.

Morris dancing in England developed from ancient weapon dances. Many Morris dances involve 'combat' with short sticks. Sword dances from northern England are similar to Morris dances, but the dancers carry swords instead of sticks. An example is the sword dance from Handsworth, just outside Sheffield. In the Handsworth dance, the eight dancers weave their swords together into a star (this is called a 'lock'). The leader of the dance then holds up the star. In other dances, the lock is put over the head of one of the dancers. The others then pull the lock apart. This movement is thought to be a **symbolic** beheading. It may have been part of a dance symbolizing the killing of winter and the arrival of spring.

Amazing Fact

Moorish dancers
In traditional Morris dances, the dancers make their faces black. Some experts think that the name 'Morris' dance comes from the Spanish *morisco* or French *moresque*, meaning Moorish (black). However, other experts think that Morris men were originally 'maris men', or Mary's men. Mary could mean the Virgin Mary, who in turn could be a substitute for older, **pagan** goddesses. Morris men probably originally blackened their faces so they would not be recognized. In many kinds of 'magic' dance, the dancers paint their faces or wear masks so that they are hard to recognize.

Technique

Swords and hoops
Belgium has a strong tradition of sword dancing. In most of the dances, swords have been replaced with sticks. In the sword dances from Westerlo (a town not far from Antwerp), the dancers carry a hoop as well as a stick. At one point they have to climb through the hoop while passing it to the next dancer, without letting go of their stick.

Another kind of sword dance involves dancing over crossed swords. Sword dancing from the Highlands in Scotland is the best-known example of this. Highland sword dances are extremely difficult and complex to perform.

A third kind of sword dance is a mock combat, either by a single dancer or between two dancers. In the sabre dance of Albania, for example, two men pretend to fight over a woman. Another example is the Highland dirk dance. This little-known dance is very different from Highland sword dancing. It is a **solo** dance in which the dancer seems to imitate the moves of a knife fight, but uses a short stick rather than a knife. Across the world in Indonesia, the Kubu people of Sumatra do a similar knife dance called the *tari pisau*.

▲ Highland sword dancing involves strong, nimble footwork and high, bouncing steps. There are many Highland sword dancing competitions, and dancers train to high levels of skill.

Technique

Capoeira and makulelê

Capoeira and makulelê are acrobatic fighting dances from Brazil. In capoeira the dancers avoid actual blows by not finishing the movement. In makulelê the dancers have sticks, which they clash together rather than hitting each other. Capoeira has become popular around the world in the last 20 years or so. However, it has turned into more of a martial art than a folk dance.

▼ Capoeira dancers stand in a circle (*roda*) around the pair who are 'fighting'. They clap and sing along with the musicians who play for the dance.

Axes, guns and sickles

Some modified sword dances use tools or other weapons instead of swords. In Cyprus, the swords are replaced with sickles, and in some dances from Afghanistan the dancers carry rifles. But not all dances involving weapons or tools are related to sword dances. In Latvia there are many stick dances in which sticks have always been used. In the past, there were wolves in this region, and men carried sticks as weapons to beat them off.

Axe dances are usually found in areas where there are forests, such as the Carpathian Mountains in eastern Europe. The axe and other weapon dances of the Carpathian region sometimes involve mock battles between two groups. The movements of the dance can be very energetic, and people are sometimes injured.

Dances from Slovakia use a long-handled axe called a *valaska*. They are all dances for men. Some are mock fights for two men, but there are also solo dances in which the dancer displays his skill, twirling his axe and jumping over it.

Work and animal dances

Folk dances in which people imitate animals seem to have existed from the earliest times. There are dances about bears, lions, bulls, stags, eagles, and less impressive animals such as magpies and frogs. Sometimes an animal is part of a hunting dance, in which a human stalks and kills the animal.

Hunting dances are dances about working. Modern folk dances include many other work dances. Many of them are to do with farming tasks, but there are also dances about weaving, spinning and making shoes.

Animal dances

Of all the different types of folk dance, animal dances are the most widespread. There are animal dances in every country. In eastern USA, the bear dance is a healing dance of the Iroquois, a Native American tribe. Other Native American tribes, such as the Mandan of the Great Plains, used to perform a bull dance to make sure the

▶ Many Australian aboriginal dances imitate animal movements. This photo shows a kangaroo dance.

herds of buffalo returned each year. In this dance, four dancers dressed in full buffalo skins and imitated buffalo movements. There are also many animal dances across Europe. In the Bourbonnais region of France, there are dances imitating the movements of several different animals. The goat dance, for instance, involves lots of leaping, while in the wolf dance the wolf sneaks about trying not to be seen. The sheep dance is a constantly changing chain dance, imitating the changing movements of a flock of sheep. In Latvia, there are dances imitating unusual animals such as magpies and frogs. The frog dance is a dance for men, in which they leap about and bounce on the ground in a 'press-up' position.

Animal dances from Asia include the Chinese lion dance (see page 35) and yak dances from northern India and Tibet. The dancer imitating the yak wears a grinning wooden mask with skulls around the top. A man rides on the dancer's back as he slowly turns and hops.

In some parts of Australia, Aborigines do kangaroo dances in which they imitate a kangaroo's movements.

Animals that look frightening are often part of dances to bring luck at New Year. The Welsh Mari Lwyd is a frightening 'horse' made from a person in a white sheet carrying a horse's skull on a pole. It goes from house to house, singing a song. At each house the Mari Lwyd gets presents of cake and money, and in return brings good luck. In Bulgaria around New Year, bands of kukeri go around the village at night. These are men dressed in frightening monster masks, and they wear bells around their waist to scare off evil spirits.

Dance Facts

The Mari Lwyd's song
There are many verses of song connected with the Mari Lywd. The song below is one example, translated from the Welsh.

> Once I was a young horse,
> And in my stable gay
> I had the best of everything
> Of barley oats and hay.
> But now I am an old horse
> My course is getting small
> I'm **'bliged** to eat the sour grass
> That grows beneath the wall.
>
> Poor old horse, let him die
> Poor old horse, let him die.
>
> I've eaten all my oats and hay
> Devoured all my straw
> I can hardly move about,
> Nor can my carriage draw.
> With these poor weary limbs of mine
> I've travelled many miles
> Over hedges, bramble bushes
> Gates and narrow stiles.
>
> Poor old horse, let him die
> Poor old horse, let him die.

▲ These stilt dancers are performing in Les Landes, France. The dancers perform each year in December.

Work dances

Many folk dances are work dances. Often, a dance imitates actions involved in farming, such as ploughing, sowing the seed, and **harvesting** the crops. In France there are dances concerned with growing and harvesting grapes, and in Slovakia there are dances about growing **hemp**. Some Russian choral dances (*khorovody*) are based around everyday work such as ploughing and sowing. The farming theme is acted out by dancers in the centre of a circle of people. The people in the circle sing a song to go with the dancing.

Shepherd's and fishermen's dances are also common working dances. An unusual shepherd's dance comes from Les Landes, in south-west France. It is done on stilts! The dance reflects the area's history, as the land was once very marshy, and shepherds used to wear stilts to avoid sinking into it. The kolyacha is a fishermen's dance from western India. The men mime the motions of rowing a fishing boat, while women wave to the men with handkerchiefs.

Although farming and fishing dances are most common, there are many others. In Provence, France, there is a weavers' dance, in which the dancers move around a wooden frame hung with ribbons. There are also shoemakers' dances, wood-cutting dances, tailors' dances and many others.

Amazing Fact

Land of the giants

One animal dance with a difference is the dance of Bayard at the Ducasse celebrations in Ath, Belgium. Every August, giant figures of **Goliath**, **Samson** and other characters parade through the streets of the city. The biggest giant of all is Bayard, a horse about 6 metres long and nearly as tall. Four children ride on Bayard's back as he dances to the sound of a brass band.

▶ Kukeri dancers from Bulgaria (shown here) and kurents dancers from Slovenia both dress in elaborate furred costumes. The kukeri and kurenti are meant to be magical animals, but the costumes are sometimes frightening.

Music and costume

The music for a folk dance can make a huge difference to how it is performed. Folk dance music varies enormously from place to place. There is also a wide variety of costumes, from very simple clothes to elaborate fancy dress.

▲ The hurdy-gurdy is a common folk instrument in France. The handle turns a wheel, which rubs against the strings and makes a sound. There are several drone strings that play single notes, as well as strings that play the melody.

The simplest music

The earliest form of folk dance music was probably singing. Some folk dances that are done today are accompanied only by singing and the noise of the dancers' feet. Most dances from Montenegro, in the Balkans, for instance, are traditionally done this way. The *khorovody* choral dances found in some parts of Russia and some Central Asian folk dances are also accompanied only by a choir.

Folk instruments

For most kinds of folk dance the instruments used are quite small and portable, since the musicians often have to move from place to place. Accordions, violins, flutes, guitars and drums are all common folk instruments.

Some countries or areas have an instrument that is characteristic of the area. Bagpipes make some Scottish music instantly recognisable. A characteristic sound of Irish music is the bodhran (a drum like a large tambourine without jingles). In Norway the Hardanger fiddle has a particular sound because of its second set of strings, which vibrate in sympathy with the main strings and produce a droning (deep humming) sound.

Different rhythms

When we listen to music we most often notice the tune first, but if we are dancing to it we notice the rhythm. Most folk music uses common rhythms, with repeating patterns of 4, 8, 3 or 6 beats. Greek folk music sometimes uses patterns of 5 and 7 beats, and in Balkan countries there can be repeating patterns of 11, 14 or 15 beats.

Even if music is in a common rhythm, it can be complex rhythmically. In Irish dancing the basic beat is divided up into many smaller sub-beats. The rhythms in some Spanish music are hard to follow because the emphasis is in unexpected places.

Dance Facts

Banned!
Tsar Peter the Great ruled Russia from 1682 to 1725. Peter wanted to modernize Russia and make it more like the countries of Western Europe. He made many useful reforms, but he also made some strange changes. For example, he banned traditional Russian musical instruments such as the balalaika and the zither, to encourage more Western-style music. The result was that people began to accompany folk dances with singing, rather than by playing instruments.

Changes in the rhythm of a dance affect the dance itself. You can see this if you compare English and American folk dances. The basic steps in many American dances are similar to those of English country dances. However, American music has different rhythms, which come from music such as jazz. The swinging beat of the music gives a very different feel to the dances.

Dressing up

Folk dances nearly always involve dressing up. In folk dance societies and performing groups, people often wear 'traditional costumes'. These are usually adaptations of what farmers and peasants in the past may have worn as their 'Sunday best'. Costumes may include embroidered skirts, dresses, waistcoats and **smocks**; aprons and shawls; all kinds of hats and headdresses; coats and jackets covered with buttons; and long socks or leggings.

Technique

Poi dance
The poi dance is a traditional Maori dance from New Zealand, Dancers carry one or two felt balls on pieces of string which they spin round as they dance. Some dances are for short poi (poi on short strings), and others are for long poi. Today poi dancing has spread around the world as a type of juggling.

▶ At performances and festivals, folk dancers often wear the traditional costumes of their country. These dancers at a midsummer festival are wearing traditional Finnish costumes.

In many kinds of folk dancing there are characters dressed up in particular ways. The Abbot's Bromley Horn Dance (see page 8), for instance, includes a **hobby horse**, a **bowman**, a **maiden** and a fool. The bowman and the maiden are often characterized as **Robin Hood** and Maid Marian. In other places dancers dress up as monsters or skeletons. In the Fastnacht carnival celebrations in south-west Germany, people wear frightening masks and dress up as witches and devils.

Many folk dances involve a prop that is used in the dance. Sometimes this is an item of clothing such as a scarf or a hat. One such dance is the jarabe tapatío, or Mexican hat dance. This is a couple dance in which the man wears a wide-brimmed hat, and the woman wears a very full, frilled skirt. Soon after the dance begins, the man tries to steal a kiss behind the hat. Later he throws it on the floor, and the pair dance round the hat. Eventually the woman picks up the hat, and the pair dance together. The woman also uses her skirt as part of the dance, swirling it around as she dances.

▲ For the Chinese Lion Dance, dancers wear stylized lion heads and elaborate costumes.

Technique

Lion dance costume
The southern lion dance comes originally from southern China and Korea. In this dance, the lion costume holds two people. The front dancer is the front legs, and also works the lion's head. The other dancer is the lion's back legs. Skilled lion dancers make the two pairs of legs seem part of one animal.

Stamping, clapping, slapping, tapping

In the Mexican hat dance (see page 35), the dancers add to the rhythms in the music by stamping and tapping their feet. This is called *zapateado*. It is just one of many kinds of stamping, clapping, tapping, clicking, jingling and tinkling noises that folk dancers make when they dance.

Step, tap, clog

Everyone knows about American tap dancing from films and musicals. Tap is not folk dance; it is a kind of show dancing. However, there were stamping and tapping folk dances long before tap was invented. Late in the 19th century, tap grew from a combination of show dance styles and Appalachian clogging. Appalachian clogging was an American folk dance, which came in turn from Irish step dancing and English clogging.

▶ As with Highland sword dancing, Irish step dancing is competitive and dancers start training at an early age. These dancers are performing in a St Patrick's Day parade in Chicago, USA.

Most people know about Irish step dancing from the musical *Riverdance*, which has been a worldwide hit since 1994. Irish step dancing is a **solo** dance style, in which the dancers perform incredibly complicated dance steps while keeping their body upright and their hands by their sides. English clogging is quite similar, but not so complex.

In some parts of *Riverdance* the dancers do almost pure Irish step dancing, but they also use ideas from other types of dance. At one point the soloist stops, then begins a tapping step very slowly. Gradually it speeds up until his feet sound like a machine-gun rattle. This is more like another kind of stamping dance – flamenco.

Spanish tap

In many kinds of Spanish folk dance, the dancers produce their own rhythms. In dances such as the *jota* and the *seguidillas*, the rhythms come from **castanets**, which the dancers play as they dance. In other dances, such as the *allegrias* and the Spanish tango, dancers stamp and tap their feet. Flamenco dance uses a combination of these different folk dance steps. What makes it different is the way in which the steps are combined with the music, singing and clapping rhythms. The dance steps are not fixed; the dancer improvises to the music and singing. The musicians also respond to what the dancer does. It is this give and take between dancers, musicians and singers that makes flamenco so complex and exciting.

▼ Flamenco dancing involves a mixture of simple folk dance steps, fast stamping and tapping steps, and liquid arm movements.

Clash and jingle

Stamping and clapping are not the only ways that folk dancers make noises. In Morris dancing, makulelê and sword dances, dancers hit sticks or swords together in rhythm with the music (see pages 24–27). In the tinikling dance from the Philippines, the dancers play a rhythm by banging two long bamboo poles together, then hitting them on the ground (see box).

Technique

Tinikling
Tinikling is a dance from the Philippines that needs fast feet and a strong nerve. Two dancers stand at either side of two long bamboo poles. Two other dancers hold the ends of the poles close to the ground. When the dance starts, the pole-holders bang the poles twice on the ground, then clap them together once. They keep this up in a regular rhythm right through the dance. The dancers step in and out between the poles, making sure to get their feet out of the way before the poles are banged together. As the dance goes on, the music and the pole banging get faster. The dancers have to be nimble on their feet to avoid getting hit!

Cymbals, pots and swords
Terah taali ('thirteen **cymbals**') is a kind of dance from Rajasthan in northern India. Dancers have a number of small cymbals fastened to their legs and arms, and they hold a cymbal in each hand. Many terah taali dances are done sitting down. The dancers swing their arms and bend their bodies to make the cymbal in their hand clash against the cymbals on their bodies in a regular rhythm. Many of the movements are imitations of everyday tasks such as spinning, weaving, grinding spices and pounding cereals into flour. In some dances the dancers wear a pot on their head, and hit their cymbals against the pot. They may also hold a sword in their teeth.

Schuhplattler
The Schuhplattler is a group of dances from the Tyrol, in the Austrian Alps. Schuhplattler dances are **courtship** dances in which the men do high jumps and kicks to show off to the women. The men also make slapping sounds by hitting themselves on the thighs, legs and feet. The men wear leather shorts, or *lederhosen*, to get a good slapping sound.

Even Morris dancers that do not use sticks wear bells on their calves, which jingle as they dance. Many Indian folk dancers also wear ankle bells, especially in northern India. Terah taali dancers from Rajasthan wear cymbals instead of bells (see box).

A Terah taalli dancer in Rajasthan dances sitting down. She clashes cymbals in her hands against others on her arms and legs.

Stories in the dance

Many kinds of folk dance originally told a story. There were stories of past battles, of how to get a girlfriend, hunting stories, animal stories, and stories about the lives of gods. In the folk dances that survive today, the stories are sometimes still there to see, but in many dances they have been lost.

Surviving stories

In a few parts of the world, folk dances still tell a clear story. Dances from Manipur in India, for example, tell stories of the Hindu god Krishna and his adventures with the Gopi, a group of cowherd **maidens**. In one story Krishna plays his flute in the forest close to where the Gopi live. The Gopi hear the beautiful music and go to find him. Krishna keeps appearing and disappearing, but eventually he joins the maidens in a circle dance in which each maiden thinks that Krishna is dancing with her alone.

▶ Manipuri is a type of folk dance from northern India. Female manipuri dances tell stories about the Hindu god Krishna, through a combination of songs and complex hand gestures.

Dance Facts

Meaningful gestures

Indian folk dances tell their stories through a number of set gestures and expressions that local audiences understand. These are simpler versions of the many rich and beautiful gestures used in Indian classical dance. The gestures were written down about 2000 years ago in a 'rule book' for Indian dance and theatre called the *Natya-sastra*.

There are other storytelling dances that are performed at particular times of year. At Easter, the Yaqui people of northern Mexico do a processional dance that combines the Christian story of Jesus's trial, death and **resurrection** with their traditional animal and hunting stories. Characters in the dance include Pontius Pilate washing his hands, wailing women, hunters, deer, coyotes and clowns.

On the other side of the world, another storytelling procession called yangko is held in north-east China to celebrate **harvest**, holidays and festivals. The procession is led by a skilled singer, who sings traditional songs but also makes up new ones. In some areas there are two yangko teams. The 'official' yangko team leader sings in praise of the area's peace and prosperity, while the 'unofficial' team leader pokes fun at local officials and events. Each person in the procession is a character from an old story, such as the monk, Monkey and Pigsy from *Journey to the West* (see below).

Dance Facts

Journey to the West

The stories in the Chinese yangko dances involve characters from an ancient Chinese story called *Journey to the West*, or sometimes just *Monkey*. In this story, the mischievous character Monkey is told by Lord Buddha to protect the monk Tripitaka on his journey to India to collect the Buddhist scriptures. Monkey is helped by two characters called Sandy and Pigsy. On the way they have many adventures, most of them involving Monkey fighting and defeating various enemies.

Lost stories

In the past it is thought that Morris dances were part of a tradition of masked story dances. Folk dances that are from this same tradition can be found across Europe, South Asia and South America. In the English Morris the idea of a story has been lost, although there are characters such as clowns, a witch doctor and a molly (a man dressed as a woman). The Italian morisca, however, the Spanish moresca dance and the matachina dance from New Mexico, USA all have the theme of a battle. These battle dances originated in 1492, when the Moors were driven out of Spain. The stories are similar to those of the English mummers' plays.

Matachina dancers in New Mexico, USA. The matachina is a dance of the Pueblo Indians. Dancers wear elaborate costumes and fight stylized battles.

Keeping the story going

Although Morris and related dances have survived, the meanings behind the dances have been lost. The same is true of many folk dances around the world. Sometimes they can seem irrelevant to life in modern towns and cities. But people around the world keep their folk dance traditions alive, even when the meaning behind them is lost. And sometimes, when you watch a folk dance or take part in it, you might feel a connection back through time to when the dance was a vital part of people's lives.

Dance Facts

Mummers' plays

Mummers' plays are a traditional custom, like folk dances. They are performed every year around Christmas time. The plays are usually funny, and they generally involve a battle between a hero (often Saint George) and a 'baddie' (sometimes called Slasher). In the battle one of the characters is killed. However, a doctor then comes along with a magic potion, and revives the dead character. The play ends with a general celebration, sometimes involving Father Christmas. The earliest complete mummers' play, published in 1779, is called *Morrice Dancers*.

▼ Mummers' plays are still performed in many parts of England. In this photo the bad character is dead and the doctor is arriving to bring him back to life.

Folk dances around the world

North America

USA, North America *Appalachian clogging, Virginia reel , square dancing, contra dancing, line dancing, Mardi Gras, sun dance, bull dance, bear dance, matachina dance*

Mexico *hat dance (jarabe tapaito), zapateado, Yaqui dances*

South America

Bolivia, Peru *traditional Andean dancing*

Brazil *capoeira, Carnival, maculelê*

Europe

Albania *sabre dance*
Austria *kolo egg dances, ländler, Schuhplattler, maypole dancing*
Balkans *kolo (circle dance)*
Belgium *Westerlo sword dance, Ducasse giant dances*
Bulgaria *kopanica, kukeri*
Carpathians *axe dances*
Cyprus *sickle dance*
Czech Republic *polka, maypole dancing*
England *maypole dancing, Morris dances, country dancing, English hey, mummers' plays, Abbots Bromley horn dance, Handsworth sword dance*
France *farandole, Borbonnais animal dances, work dances, Provence moresque, shepherd's stilt dance*
Germany *ländler, maypole dancing, Fastnacht carnival*

Ireland *Puck Fair, Irish reels, Irish step dancing, fire festivals*
Italy *wedding sword dances (north), morisca*
Latvia *stick dances, frog dance, magpie dance*
Lithuania *axe dance*
Norway *halling*
Poland *Matthew is dead*
Pyrenees *Basque dancing*
Romania *capra (goat dance), hora (circle dances)*
Russia *plyaska, khorovody (choral dances)*
Scotland *Highland sword dancing, Highland dirk dance, Scottish country dance, fire festivals*
Slovakia *circle dances, valaska, axe dances, wedding dances*
Spain *Flamenco, fandango, moresca, jota, seguidillas, sardana*
Sweden *maypole dancing*
Wales *Mari Lwyd, fire festivals*

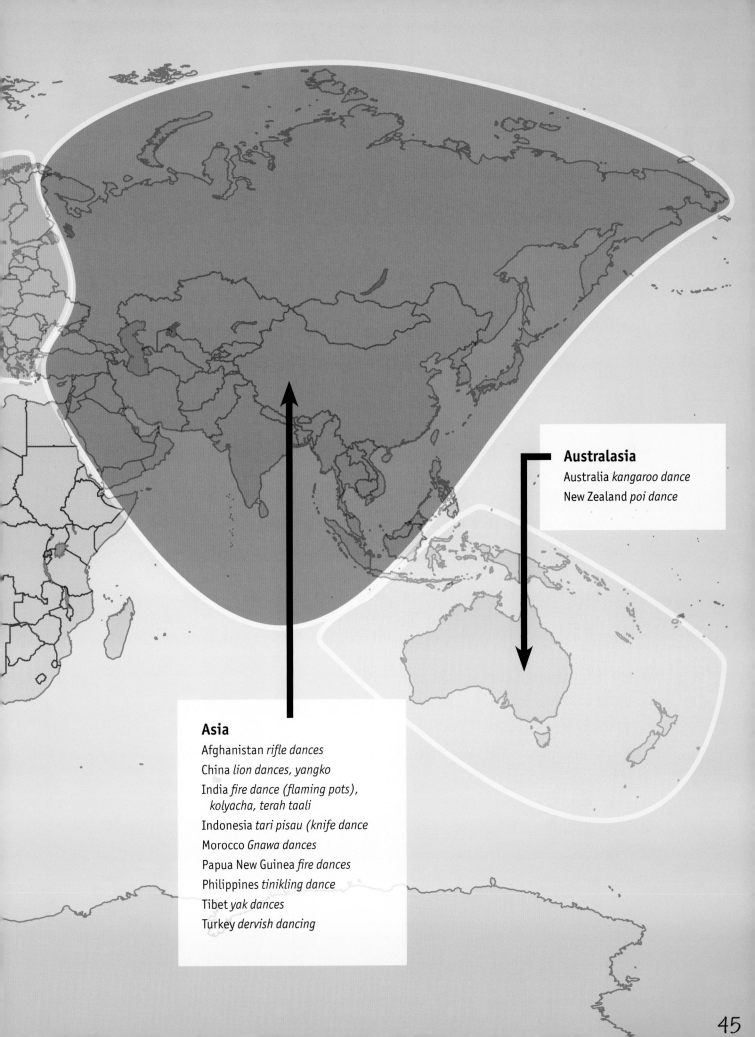

Australasia
Australia *kangaroo dance*
New Zealand *poi dance*

Asia
Afghanistan *rifle dances*
China *lion dances, yangko*
India *fire dance (flaming pots),
    kolyacha, terah taali*
Indonesia *tari pisau (knife dance*
Morocco *Gnawa dances*
Papua New Guinea *fire dances*
Philippines *tinikling dance*
Tibet *yak dances*
Turkey *dervish dancing*

Glossary

'bliged short for obliged (have to do something)

bowman archer

castanets Spanish percussion instrument that can be played with one hand. It makes a clacking sound when the two halves are hit together.

courtship when a boy and girl, or a man and a woman, like each other and go out together

cymbal circular metal percussion instrument that makes a clashing sound when hit or when two of them are hit against each other

descendant related in a direct line to someone or something in the past

Goliath giant man in a story from the Bible

harvest time when main farm crops such as wheat or rice are ripe and are cut down (harvested)

hemp fibrous plant material used to make things such as rope

hobby horse a toy: a horse's head on a stick, often with wheels, that can be used as a pretend horse

improvise make things up on the spot

maiden young, unmarried woman

pagan often used to mean any religious belief that is not part of the four main religions (Buddhism, Christianity, Hinduism and Islam)

prop (short for 'property') object that is used on stage

resurrection when someone who was dead comes alive again

ritual solemn ceremony that happens according to a set plan

Robin Hood character in English legend who robbed from the rich to give to the poor

sacrifice kill an animal or human for religious reasons

Samson extremely strong man in a story from the Bible

smock a loose shirt or overall worn by peasants in the past to protect their clothes

solo dance performed by one person

symbolic acting as a symbol of something. Something that stands for something else

wreath small circular decoration made of flowers or leaves

Further information

Books

Kariamu Welsh Asante, *African Dance (World of Dance)*. Chelsea House Publishers (2004)

Sherry Bonnice, *Folk Dance (North American Folklore)*. Mason Crest Publishers (2002)

Rita Storey, *Irish Dancing and other National Dances (Get Dancing)*. Sea to Sea Publications (2007)

F. Isabel Campoy and Alma Flor Ada, *Celebrate Cinco de Mayo with the Mexican Hat Dance*. Alfaguara Infantil (2006)

Films

Flamenco. A film by Spanish director Carlos Saura that shows a wide range of different flamenco dancers and musicians.

Soy Andina. A documentary by Canadian film-maker Mitch Teplitsky about two very different women from New York going to Peru and getting involved in Andean folk dance.

Websites

Examples of many of the dances in the book can be found on the YouTube website.

www.artsalive.ca/en/dan/dance101/forms.asp#afro-caribbean
Information about dance from many countries.

www.dunav.org.il/index.html
This website has lots of information about Balkan folk dancing.

www.bekkoame.ne.jp/~noriks/ENGLISH/514100e.html
Animations help you to learn the basic steps and patterns of square dancing.

www.aca-dla.org/dlamusic/dlamusic.html
If you want to hear what real 'old-timey' music sounds like, explore this website.

www.efdss.org/history.htm
History of the oldest folk society in the world, the English Folk Dance and Song Society.

www.traditionalmusic.co.uk/appalachian-clogging/appalachian-clogging-01.htm
A website where you can learn the basic steps of Appalachian clog dancing.

Index